The Sanctuary in Types and Symbols

Doug Clemmerson

TEACH Services, Inc.
PUBLISHING
www.TEACHServices.com • (800) 367-1844

World rights reserved. This book or any portion thereof may not be copied or reproduced in any form or manner whatever, except as provided by law, without the written permission of the publisher, except by a reviewer who may quote brief passages in a review.

The author assumes full responsibility for the accuracy of all facts and quotations as cited in this book. The opinions expressed in this book are the author's personal views and interpretations, and do not necessarily reflect those of the publisher.

This book is provided with the understanding that the publisher is not engaged in giving spiritual, legal, medical, or other professional advice. If authoritative advice is needed, the reader should seek the counsel of a competent professional.

Copyright © 2021 Doug Clemmerson
Copyright © 2021 TEACH Services, Inc.
ISBN-13: 978-1-4796-1130-0 (Paperback)
ISBN-13: 978-1-4796-1131-7 (ePub)
Library of Congress Control Number: 2021911869

Unless otherwise indicated, Scripture references are taken from the King James Version of the Bible.

Scripture labeled (NKJV) is taken from the New King James Version®. Copyright © 1982 by Thomas Nelson. Used by permission. All rights reserved.

Scripture labeled (NASB) is taken from the NEW AMERICAN STANDARD BIBLE®, Copyright © 1960,1962,1963,1968,1971,1972,1973,1975,1977,1995 by The Lockman Foundation. Used by permission.

If you would like to contact the author, enter the links below in your web browser:
e-mail: https://1ref.us/re9456929
Phone: https://1ref.us/rp9456929

Published by

TEACH Services, Inc.
P U B L I S H I N G
www.TEACHServices.com • (800) 367-1844

Table of Contents

Introduction	v
Chapter 1—What Is the Sanctuary?	9
Chapter 2—What Do the Materials Used For the Building Of the Sanctuary Represent?	11
Chapter 3—What Do the Colors and Materials Represent In the Bible?	17
Chapter 4—Quotes on Fine Linen by Ellen G. White	27
Chapter 5—Further Discussion on Colors and Coverings	31
Chapter 6—What Does Goat's Hair Represent In the Bible?	35
Chapter 7—What Do Rams' Skins Dyed Red Represent In the Bible?	39
Chapter 8—What Do Badgers' Skins Represent In the Bible?	43
Chapter 9—What Does Acacia Wood Symbolize In the Bible?	45
Chapter 10—An Illustration of Christ's Incarnation	51
Chapter 11—The Finished Work	55
Chapter 12—A Partial Picture of Jesus	63
Chapter 13—What Does Oil Symbolize In the Bible?	69
Chapter 14—The Ephod and the Breastplate	77
Bibliography	80

Introduction

What is the sanctuary spoken of in the Bible? It is often referred to as the tabernacle. The reason why it is called by this name is that, in Hebrew, it means "dwelling place," and God commanded Moses to build a tabernacle so that He could "dwell," i.e., live, among the children of Israel.

What is interesting is that when Moses was on top of Mount Sinai receiving the Ten Commandments, which God Himself wrote upon two tables of stone, he also saw in a vision the sanctuary in heaven. God told Moses to be sure to build the earthly tabernacle according to the pattern he was shown in the mountain.

The question then is, Why would the God of heaven, the Creator of the universe, want to dwell among us sinful human beings? It may seem hard to accept, but the fact of the matter is that He loves us even more than life itself. Ever since the separation that took place in the Garden of Eden, when Adam and Eve sinned and ate of the tree of knowledge of good and evil, our Creator has longed to restore that bond that we, by our disobedience, broke.

As we dig deeper into our study on the sanctuary and its services, it is my prayer that all of us will be blessed and benefited by these precious revelations of God's love and plan to save us from our sins and restore His divine image in us, which iniquity has well-nigh obliterated.

At the time when the children of Israel came upon the scene of earth's history, God made a covenant with their forefathers, Abraham, Isaac, and Jacob (whom He renamed Israel later on in his life). To them, He committed the privilege of being His chosen people, revealing His character to those whom Satan had steeped in paganism and idolatry, and witnessing to a lost and dying world of the love of God for humanity.

As we dig deeper into our study on the sanctuary and its services, it is my prayer that all of us will be blessed and benefited by these precious revelations of God's love and plan to save us from our sins and restore His divine image in us, which iniquity has well-nigh obliterated.

God bless each and every one of us, and may we, at the end of this study, open our hearts fully to Jesus and allow Him to "dwell" in us by faith and perfect His character in us, that we can be fitted to dwell with Him forever in the new heavens and earth that He has promised to make.

Chapter 1—What Is the Sanctuary?

And let them make me a sanctuary; that I may dwell among them. According to all that I shew thee, *after* **the pattern of the tabernacle, and the pattern of all the instruments thereof, even so shall ye make** *it***. … And look that thou make** *them* **after their pattern, which was shewed thee in the mount. (Exodus 25:8, 9, 40)**

In this first part, we are going to get a brief overview of the sanctuary, describing the construction and furniture of this artifice, as well as its services. We are going to be reading a lot from the Bible on this vital subject. It is my prayer that we will all be blessed and benefited by these magnificent truths.

Also, I would like to let everyone know this is NOT copyrighted material. Please feel free to share it on your Facebook pages and even copy, print, and share it in your local churches and with friends and family. WE STRONGLY ENCOURAGE THIS!

And the LORD spake unto Moses, saying, Speak unto the children of Israel, that they bring me an offering: of every man that giveth it willingly with his heart ye shall take my offering. And this *is* **the offering which ye shall take of them; gold, and silver, and brass, And blue, and purple, and scarlet, and fine linen, and goats'** *hair***, And rams' skins dyed red, and badgers' skins, and shittim wood, Oil for the light, spices for anointing oil, and for sweet incense, Onyx stones, and stones to be set in the ephod, and in the breastplate. (Exodus 25:1–7)**

It is important to note that in verse 2, God told Moses to tell the children of Israel that those who would give offerings to help with the construction of the sanctuary were to do so with a willing heart. Why would He say this? Because our heavenly Father has created each one of us with a free will to choose and will never force us to do anything that we don't want to do.

It is also the same today when it comes to accepting Christ's sacrifice on Calvary's cross for our sins and living the Christian life. If we choose to not willfully accept what Jesus has done for us, God honors our choice, even though He knows it's not for our good. He loves us and wants us to choose to surrender our hearts and lives to Him willfully, out of love, for what He has done for us in giving His Son to die.

God even tells us in the Bible that He wants us to give our hearts to Him and observe His ways **(see Proverbs 23:26)** because He knows us better than we know ourselves and that no matter how hard we try to change ourselves, we can't stop doing things that are not good for us. Jesus Himself said, "For without Me you can do nothing" (John 15:5, NKJV). Again, God says this to us: Can the Ethiopian change his skin, or the leopard his spots? *then* may ye also do good, that are accustomed to do evil (Jeremiah 13:23).

> *We see that it is impossible for us to change ourselves. Only Jesus can do this for us. We also need to realize that it is only by surrendering our lives and hearts to Him that we can ever be assured of heaven and not allow Satan to continue to deceive us into thinking that we can get there by some other means.*

We see that it is impossible for us to change ourselves. Only Jesus can do this for us. We also need to realize that it is only by surrendering our lives and hearts to Him that we can ever be assured of heaven and not allow Satan to continue to deceive us into thinking that we can get there by some other means. Listen to what Jesus says to us in the following verses. **"Jesus saith unto him, I am the way, the truth, and the life: no man cometh unto the Father, but by Me" (John 14:6). "I am the door: by me if any man enter in, he shall be saved, and shall go in and out, and find pasture" (10:9).**

As we continue our study on the sanctuary, we will discover what Jesus meant by these passages, and it will help us see, not only what we need to do to accept Jesus as our Lord and Savior, but also how to prepare ourselves for His soon coming. In our next part, we will be discussing the symbolism of the materials used to make the curtains, coverings, and furniture of the sanctuary and what they mean.

Chapter 2—What Do the Materials Used For the Building Of the Sanctuary Represent?

In our first section, we discovered what the sanctuary was, as well as its purpose. Now in this section, we will go into detail about the materials used in constructing the sanctuary and what they symbolize. And as we continue, we are going to discover many wonderful truths that even the building itself reveal to us about how the whole plan of salvation was laid out in heaven before the creation of our world and its inhabitants. We will also discover the cause of the great controversy, in which every one of us is involved, and how to be on the winning side.

The materials (ref. Exodus 25:1–9) are listed precisely as God had specified, nothing more and nothing less, because they would each have specific, symbolic meaning relating to the true sanctuary in heaven and Jesus Christ. Nothing could be left to chance or mankind's imagination because if the Lord is to dwell here and pitch His **tent** with humanity, then they are to approach Him His way, with no exceptions.

The details of its construction would pattern, in a temporal way, what God would one day do permanently through Jesus Christ. The sanctuary would become a visible model of how we come to the Father through the Son. Let's now look at the materials to be used in the construction of the tabernacle and keep in mind that we must examine the symbolism against a Hebraic backdrop. The Old Testament is filled with figurative language that can be interpreted in the light of its context.

Materials (Ordered by God)

Gold (Deity)

According to Exodus 38, they gave approximately 2,100 pounds of gold. Pure Gold throughout the Scriptures speaks of divinity, that which cannot be reproduced by mankind. Gold is made by God and comes down from Him. It speaks of the deity of Jesus Christ and typifies His divine glory as the Son of God and God the Son.

Jesus was none other than Yahweh in the flesh. He is *Malak Yahweh*—Angel of the Lord. When Isaiah saw the Lord high and lifted up as the

King in all His glory, John, in the New Testament, told us that it was Jesus whom he saw. "In the year that king Uzziah died I saw also the Lord sitting upon a throne, high and lifted up, and his train filled the temple" (Isaiah 6:1). "These things Isaiah said when he saw His glory and spoke of Him" (John 12:41, NKJV).

> *Our character is the gold tried in the fire. It is achieved through receiving the Holy Spirit as He writes the law in our hearts. It is what makes all we do spiritual and acceptable. It is the motives and intentions behind all our actions. It is rooted in the law and acted out in love.*

Gold represents the One with a perfect character. All furniture in the Holy Place and Most Holy Place and the walls of the sanctuary were gold. Everything represents the recognition of the perfection of Christ after He had left the earth (outer court). While He was on earth, He was treated as a man of common metal and even Satan himself.

Gold also represents the perfection of Christ's character fully reflected in His people. For example, consider the counsel given to the Laodiceans. "I counsel thee to buy of me gold tried in the fire, that thou mayest be rich; and white raiment, that thou mayest be clothed, and *that* the shame of thy nakedness do not appear; and anoint thine eyes with eyesalve, that thou mayest see" **(Revelation 3:18).**

Furthermore, gold signifies character. Our character is the gold tried in the fire. It is achieved through receiving the Holy Spirit as He writes the law in our hearts. It is what makes all we do spiritual and acceptable. It is the motives and intentions behind all our actions. It is rooted in the law and acted out in love.

Gold can also symbolize the following: perfection, faith, and love tried in the fire.

> And he shall sit *as* a refiner and purifier of silver: and he shall purify the sons of Levi, and purge them as gold and silver, that they may offer unto the Lord an offering in righteousness. (Malachi 3:3)
>
> Now if any man build upon this foundation gold, silver, precious stones, wood, hay, stubble; Every man's work shall be made manifest: for the day shall declare it, because it shall be revealed by fire; and the fire shall try every man's work of what sort it is. If any

man's work abide which he hath built thereupon, he shall receive a reward. If any man's work shall be burned, he shall suffer loss: but he himself shall be saved; yet so as by fire. (1 Corinthians 3:12–15)

Silver (Redemption)
The silver came to approximately 7,300 pounds. Throughout the Scriptures, silver figuratively speaks of redemption. It was always used as redemption money. **"And thou shalt take the atonement money of the children of Israel, and shalt appoint it for the service of the tabernacle of the congregation; that it may be a memorial unto the children of Israel before the Lord, to make an atonement for your souls" (Exodus 30:16).**

The sanctuary stood upon sockets of silver. Both Joseph and Jesus were sold for silver. Judas was paid off in silver, as the Scriptures say. Silver is redemption money. It is symbolic of the redemption that comes through Jesus Christ alone. It prefigures the preciousness of Christ as the ransom for sinners. Notice that there is no silver mentioned in heaven. The people will have already been redeemed. "For even the Son of man came not to be ministered unto, but to minister, and to give his life a ransom for many" (Mark 10:45).

Silver can also symbolize the following: obedience, redemption, and prayer.

> When thou takest the sum of the children of Israel after their number, then shall they give every man a ransom for his soul unto the Lord, when thou numberest them; that there be no plague among them, when *thou* numberest them. (Exodus 30:12)
>
> And thy estimation shall be of the male from twenty years old even unto sixty years old, even thy estimation shall be fifty shekels of silver, after the shekel of the sanctuary. (Leviticus 27:3)
>
> As a wise master builder, Jeremiah at the very beginning of his lifework sought to encourage the men of Judah to lay the foundations of their spiritual life broad and deep, by making thorough work of repentance. Long had they been building with material likened by the apostle Paul to wood, hay, and stubble, and by Jeremiah himself to dross. "Refuse silver shall men call them," he declared of the impenitent nation, "because the Lord hath rejected them." Jeremiah 6:30, margin. Now they were urged to begin building wisely and for eternity, casting aside the rubbish of apostasy and unbelief, and using as foundation material the pure gold, the

refined silver, the precious stones--faith and obedience and good works--which alone are acceptable in the sight of a holy God. (White, *Prophets and Kings*, pp. 409, 410)

Bronze (Judgment)

Approximately 600 pounds of **bronze** was given for use in those places where exceptional strength and heat resistance was important. Bronze has a melting point of about 1,700 degrees Fahrenheit. It was necessary for the altar of burnt offering because it was located outside, where intense heat was present. They brought bronze, not brass. Brass comes from a mixture of copper and zinc, whereas bronze comes from copper and tin.

Bronze represents judgment. When Moses raised the bronze serpent, it spoke of the power of the devil being judged through the raising of the Son of God. "And Moses made a serpent of brass, and put it upon a pole, and it came to pass, that if a serpent had bitten any man, when he beheld the serpent of brass, he lived" (Numbers 21:9). Christ, suffering as a wicked man in the outer court, was represented as a bronze snake and the sin offering on the bronze altar, with a bronze laver holding the water of cleansing.

Bronze typifies the divine character of Christ, who took upon Himself the fire of God's wrath, holiness, and justice by becoming a **sin offering.** The furniture in the outer court and the base of the poles were made of bronze, which is not a pure metal. It represents our mixed state on earth as we are joined to God through the Holy Spirit. It is the metal that is used for fiery trials and to symbolize the cleansing that the righteous must go through on the earth. We will all be washed by water; we must all pass through the fire.

> Every thing that may abide the fire, ye shall make *it* go through the fire, and it shall be clean: nevertheless it shall be purified with the water of separation: and all that abideth not the fire ye shall make go through the water. (Numbers 31:23)
>
> For we are labourers together with God: ye are God's husbandry, *ye are* God's building. According to the grace of God which is given unto me, as a wise masterbuilder, I have laid the foundation, and another buildeth thereon. But let every man take heed how he buildeth thereupon. For other foundation can no man lay than that is laid, which is Jesus Christ. (1 Corinthians 3:9–11)

Bronze can also symbolize the following: strength, endurance, the victory gained through suffering, and judgment.

> And of Asher he said, *Let* Asher *be* blessed with children; let him be acceptable to his brethren, and let him dip his foot in oil. Thy shoes *shall be* iron and brass; and as thy days, *so shall* thy strength *be*. (Deuteronomy 33:24, 25)
>
> And I turned, and lifted up mine eyes, and looked, and, behold, there came four chariots out from between two mountains; and the mountains *were* mountains of brass. (Zechariah 6:1)
>
> Him that overcometh will I make a pillar in the temple of my God, and he shall go no more out: and I will write upon him the name of my God, and the name of the city of my God, *which is* new Jerusalem, which cometh down out of heaven from my God: and *I will write upon him* my new name. (Revelation 3:12)
>
> And I will break the pride of your power; and I will make your heaven as iron, and your earth as brass. (Leviticus 26:19)
>
> And the LORD said unto Moses, Make thee a fiery serpent, and set it upon a pole: and it shall come to pass, that every one that is bitten, when he looketh upon it, shall live. And Moses made a serpent of brass, and put it upon a pole, and it came to pass, that if a serpent had bitten any man, when he beheld the serpent of brass, he lived. (Numbers 21:8, 9)

Chapter 3—What Do the Colors and Materials Represent In the Bible?

Blue

"And they saw the God of Israel: and there was under his feet as it were a paved work of a sapphire stone, and as it were the body of heaven in his clearness" (Exodus 24:10).

> And above the firmament that *was* over their heads *was* the likeness of a throne, as the appearance of a sapphire stone: and upon the likeness of the throne *was* the likeness as the appearance of a man above upon it. (Ezekiel 1:26)
>
> Speak unto the children of Israel, and bid them that they make them fringes in the borders of their garments throughout their generations, and that they put upon the fringe of the borders a ribband of blue: And it shall be unto you for a fringe, that ye may look upon it, and remember all the commandments of the LORD, and do them; and that ye seek not after your own heart and your own eyes, after which ye use to go a whoring: That ye may remember, and do all my commandments, and be holy unto your God. I *am* the LORD your God, which brought you out of the land of Egypt, to be your God: I *am* the LORD your God. (Numbers 15:38–41)

Blue represents the law. The Ten Commandments were carved from a blue stone that was a part of the throne of God. The Israelites wore a blue tassel to remind them of the law. The priest's garment had gold, red, blue, and purple. The whore of revelation was adorned in everything except blue; she violates the law, yet wants riches, priesthood, and sacrifice. She just did not like the rules. However, we are a people of the law.

The Question of God's Supremacy Settled

"Lift up your heads, O ye gates; and be ye lift up, ye everlasting doors; and the King of glory shall come in" (Ps. 24:7).

All heaven is watching the controversy. ... Here upon the earth Satan stirs up the enmity that is in the human mind to resist the salvation that has been brought to them at such an infinite cost. He [Christ] was the light of the world, and yet the world knew Him not. He created the world, and yet the world would not acknowledge Him. But when His life was sought for, the Majesty of heaven had to go from place to place; heaven marked this. And He was despised and rejected; He was mocked at, reviled; but when He was reviled, He reviled not again. But Satan did not stop his persecutions until Christ hung upon the cross of Calvary. All heaven, and all the worlds God had created, were watching the controversy; would Christ carry out the plan He had undertaken to lift lost souls from the pit of sin? ...

The great rebel was uprooted from the thoughts of everyone as they saw Christ's resurrection; the question was settled that the law of God was immutable and covered all that were in heaven and in earth, and all the created intelligences. Christ was with His disciples forty days and forty nights and then ... He was taken up from them into heaven; and the multitude of captives were with Him; and a multitude of heavenly host was around Him; and as they approached the city of God, the angel that was accompanying Him said, "Lift up your heads, O ye gates; and be ye lifted up, ye everlasting doors; and the King of glory shall come in." ...

Now this Saviour is our intercessor, making an atonement for us before the Father... And that precious Saviour is coming again. ... When He cometh the second time, it is not to wear the crown of thorns, it is not to have that old purple robe placed upon His divine form. The voices will not be raised, Crucify Him, Crucify Him, but there is a shout from the angelic host and from those who are waiting to receive Him, Worthy, Worthy is the Lamb that was slain. A divine Conqueror, in the place of the crown of thorns He will wear a crown of glory; in the place of that old kingly robe that they put upon Him in mockery, He will wear a robe whiter than the whitest white. And those hands that were bruised with the cruel nails will shine like gold. ...

The righteous dead come forth from their graves, and they that are alive and remain are caught up together with them to meet the Lord in the air, and so shall they ever be with the Lord. And they will listen to the voice of Jesus, sweeter than any music that ever fell on mortal ear, ... "Come, ye blessed of my Father, inherit the kingdom prepared for you from the foundation of the world." (White, *Christ Triumphant*, p. 288)

Purple

In this section of our study on the materials and colors used for the coverings of the sanctuary, we are going to find out what the color **purple** represents. **Purple covered the altar of burnt offering.** "Then they shall take away the ashes from the altar, and spread a purple cloth over it" (Numbers 4:13, NASB).

Purple has become the symbol of royalty, but it was clearly a symbol that was related to the priesthood and sacrifice when God used it. This color was in the priest's garments, as well as the coverings of the sanctuary and doorways. Significantly, the altar of sacrifice was covered in purple when the sanctuary was moved. There was a prophetic import that was fulfilled when Jesus was dressed in purple at the trial. "And the soldiers twisted together a crown of thorns and put it on His head, and put a purple robe on Him" (John 19:2, NASB; see also Mark 15:17).

The priest is the lawyer for the government and law of God. He studies this law, teaches it to the people, and administers justice. Therefore, Christ becomes our priest and defender before God. The color purple is in the doors to the sanctuary because it is the place where we go to get justice from God. It is the color of the royal priesthood.

In a secular context, since purple was expensive to produce, it became

> *Purple is a combination of red and blue. Jesus fulfilled the demands of the law by becoming the sacrifice. He atoned for the broken law (blue) with His red blood. Therefore, when the law and sacrifice combined, it formed royalty.*

associated with wealth. The emperors of Rome eventually used this color for royalty. Therefore, at the time of Jesus' trial, the soldiers intended to mock Him as the king of the Jews, dressing Him in purple and placing a crown of thorns on His head. When they did this, they inadvertently dressed Him up as the altar of sacrifice. So, although they intended to mock Him, they unknowingly fulfilled a prophecy as they dressed the altar for transportation.

Purple is a combination of red and blue. Jesus fulfilled the demands of the law by becoming the sacrifice. He atoned for the broken law (blue) with His red blood. Therefore, when the law and sacrifice combined, it formed royalty. No wonder the place of sacrifice was covered in purple! We are also destined to be priest-kings (and queens) of God by dying daily to sin.

Red (Scarlet)

In this section of our study on the materials and colors used for the coverings of the sanctuary, we are going to find out what the color **red** represents. "For the life of the flesh *is* in the blood" (Leviticus 17:11). Red is the sacrifice. It means life. When life is taken, red can appear to mean death. It is the blood of Christ that cleanses us and covers us from the penalty of sin.

The sanctuary had a covering of red. This symbolizes the protection that the blood of Christ offers us. This covering is the mercy seat over us. This dimension points out a characteristic of heaven. We are connected. If one suffers, all suffer. We bear each other's burdens. We give, no matter the cost. Receiving is just a bonus. What we are about is the welfare of others. We are sacrificial people. Just as Jesus died and shed His blood to give life to the world, we are to share this precious story with others.

Therefore, when then we see the covering of the sanctuary that had the curtain with the ram's skins dyed red, it represented a substitutionary sacrifice, which clearly points forward to the death of our Lord Jesus for the sins of the world. It was also to remind the children of Israel that the only true cleansing for sin was to be found in the death of Christ alone.

Scarlet Thread (Sacrifice)

The scarlet was derived from an Eastern insect (worm; see Psalm 22:6) that infests certain trees. It was gathered, crushed, dried, and ground to a powder that produced a brilliant crimson hue. Scarlet speaks of sacrifice and typifies Christ in His sufferings. He somehow took upon Himself a body of flesh and blood and then died, giving His life as a ransom for us all by being crushed in the mills of God's justice.

Chapter 3

"And walk in love, as Christ also hath loved us, and hath given himself for us an offering and a sacrifice to God for a sweetsmelling savour" (Ephesians 5:2).

"For then must he often have suffered since the foundation of the world: but now, once in the end of the world hath he appeared to put away sin by the sacrifice of himself" (Hebrews 9:26).

One may ask, "Why is that?" The answer is simple:

> For *it is* not possible that the blood of bulls and of goats should take away sins. Wherefore when he cometh into the world, he saith, Sacrifice and offering thou wouldest not, but a body hast thou prepared me: In burnt offerings and *sacrifices* for sin thou hast had no pleasure. Then said I, Lo, I come (in the volume of the book it is written of me,) to do thy will, O God. Above when he said, Sacrifice and offering and burnt offerings and *offering* for sin thou wouldest not, neither hadst pleasure *therein*; which are offered by the law; Then said he, Lo, I come to do thy will, O God. He taketh away the first, that he may establish the second. By the which will we are sanctified through the offering of the body of Jesus Christ once *for all*. (Hebrews 10:4–10)

From these verses, we can see that the only way to truly bring an end to sin and for us weak, erring, mortal human beings to be able to resist the lures and enticements of Satan and the transgressions he tempts us all to commit was for our Lord Jesus to step down from His throne in heaven. You see friends, He willfully left the companionship of holy beings, came to our dark, sin-laden world, and lived among us, enduring the temptations that the devil brought upon Him with such fierceness and intensity. Satan did all of this in hopes of causing Jesus our Creator to sin so that the human race and all possibilities of redeeming us from the curse of the law (which is iniquity) would be lost.

However, praise be to God that our Lord Jesus never yielded to any of the temptations of Satan, not even once. Even with Him having our fallen, sinful nature, Jesus still came off victorious. How and why? Because He didn't trust in His own strength or use His divinity to overcome, but trusted in the Father and His Word. Every time, Jesus overcame the enemy's temptations by quoting the Bible. In doing this, He has left us an example, and if we are to be victorious over sin and the enticements of the enemy, we must rely upon divine strength and the Word of God, not in ourselves or our weak, finite power.

Wherewithal shall a young man cleanse his way? by taking heed *thereto* according to thy word. ... Thy word have I hid in mine heart, that I might not sin against thee. (Psalm 119:9, 11)

Then was Jesus led up of the Spirit into the wilderness to be tempted of the devil. And when he had fasted forty days and forty nights, he was afterward an hungered. And when the tempter came to him, he said, If thou be the Son of God, command that these stones be made bread. But he answered and said, It is written, Man shall not live by bread alone, but by every word that proceedeth out of the mouth of God. Then the devil taketh him up into the holy city, and setteth him on a pinnacle of the temple, And saith unto him, If thou be the Son of God, cast thyself down: for it is written, He shall give his angels charge concerning thee: and in *their* hands they shall bear thee up, lest at any time thou dash thy foot against a stone. Jesus said unto him, It is written again, Thou shalt not tempt the Lord thy God. Again, the devil taketh him up into an exceeding high mountain, and sheweth him all the kingdoms of the world, and the glory of them; And saith unto him, All these things will I give thee, if thou wilt fall down and worship me. Then saith Jesus unto him, Get thee hence, Satan: for it is written, Thou shalt worship the Lord thy God, and him only shalt thou serve. (Matthew 4:1–10)

White (Fine Linen)

In this section of our study on the materials and colors used for the coverings of the sanctuary, we are going to find out what **white (fine linen)** represents. We are also going to share several quotes from Ellen G. White that, along with the Bible, will help us more clearly understand to what the fine linen in Exodus 25:4 is really referring, and how vital it is to all of us if we expect to be allowed to enter in through the gates of the New Jerusalem.

It is my continued prayer that as we progress further along in this study, all of us will be drawn closer to our Lord Jesus and more fully surrendered to Him than we have ever been before. May all who read and study this booklet on the sanctuary be blessed, rooted, and grounded firmly in the truth like never before, with our feet firmly planted upon the Rock of our salvation, our Lord Jesus Christ.

Come now, and let us reason together, saith the Lord though your sins be as scarlet, they shall be as white as snow; though they be red like crimson, they shall be as wool. (Isaiah 1:18)

And to her was granted that she should be arrayed in fine linen, clean and white: for the fine linen is the righteousness of saints. (Revelation 19:8)

Behold, I come as a thief. Blessed *is* he that watcheth, and keepeth his garments, lest he walk naked, and they see his shame. (Revelation 16:15)

Thou hast a few names even in Sardis which have not defiled their garments; and they shall walk with me in white: for they are worthy. (Revelation 3:4)

And unto the angel of the church of the Laodiceans write; These things saith the Amen, the faithful and true witness, the beginning of the creation of God; I know thy works, that thou art neither cold nor hot: I would thou wert cold or hot. So then because thou art lukewarm, and neither cold nor hot, I will spue thee out of my mouth. Because thou sayest, I am rich, and increased with goods, and have need of nothing; and knowest not that thou art wretched, and miserable, and poor, and blind, and naked: I counsel thee to buy of me gold tried in the fire, that thou mayest be rich; and white raiment, that thou mayest be clothed, and that the shame of thy nakedness do not appear; and anoint thine eyes with eyesalve, that thou mayest see. As many as I love, I rebuke and chasten: be zealous therefore, and repent. Behold, I stand at the door, and knock: if any man hear my voice, and open the door, I will come in to him, and will sup with him, and he with me. To him that overcometh will I grant to sit with me in my throne, even as I also overcame, and am set down with my Father in his throne. He that hath an ear, let him hear what the Spirit saith unto the churches. (Revelation 3:14–22)

It is the covenant that joins the law and love. It is grace that combines sacrifice with love to give us pardon. It is love that causes mercy to be patient while our characters develop. Through Christ, we are complete people.

The Glory of God

The evidence suggests that when we obtain this perfect balance of colors in our characters, it will also appear in a physical form. The glory of God appears as a white, shining light that radiates from the body as the spiritual and physical fully unite. Goodness is glory and can be seen and put on like clothes. "And he said, I beseech thee, shew me thy glory. And he said, I will make all my goodness pass before thee, and I will proclaim the name of the Lord before thee; and will be gracious to whom I will be gracious, and will shew mercy on whom I will shew mercy" (Exodus 33:18, 19).

The color **white** in Scripture is translated from the Hebrew words *laban* or *chivvah*, meaning "white"; *buwts* means "white linen"; *byssus* is a costly, fine white linen cloth made in Egypt; *tsach* means "white, dazzling, glowing, clear, bright."

The Greek words are *leukos*, meaning "white, light, bright, brilliant from whiteness"; *leukaino* meaning "to make white" or "to whiten."

"And I said unto him, Sir, thou knowest. And he said to me, These are they which came out of great tribulation, and have washed their robes, and made them white in the blood of the Lamb" (Revelation 7:14).

> *Only after learning the basic principles of Scripture can the disciple of Christ move on to understand the deeper principles and spiritual lessons thereof.*

And [Jesus'] raiment became shining, exceeding white as snow; so as no fuller on earth can white them" (Mark 9:3).

God fed the Israelites during their journey through the desert after bringing them out of Egypt. "And the house of Israel called its name Manna. And it *was* like white coriander seed, and the taste of it *was* like wafers *made* with honey" (Exodus 16:31, NKJV). This white substance represented a profound, spiritual lesson: that "man shall not live by bread alone; but man lives by every word that proceeds from the mouth of the Lord" (Deuteronomy. 8:3, NKJV).

The whiteness of milk is associated with the basic principles and teachings of God's Word. "And I, brethren, could not speak to you as to spiritual *people* but as to carnal, as to babes in Christ. I fed you with milk and not with solid food; for until now you were not able *to receive it*, and even now you are still not able" (1 Corinthians 3:1, 2, NKJV). Only after learning the basic principles of Scripture can the disciple of Christ move on to understand the deeper principles and spiritual lessons thereof.

In Scripture, white is connected with purity and righteousness. In Roman times, the giving of a white stone symbolized acquittal from crime—innocence. Thus, those who overcome sin are purified and cleansed through faith in the Lord Jesus Christ. "Purge me with hyssop, and I shall be clean: wash me, and I shall be whiter than snow" (Psalm 51:7). "He that hath an ear, let him hear what the Spirit saith unto the churches; To him that overcometh will I give to eat of the hidden manna, and will give him a white stone, and in the stone a new name written, which no man knoweth saving he that receiveth it" (Revelation 2:17).

In ancient times, a white stone was used in court to symbolize innocence and purity, while a black one symbolized guilt. Jesus promised that the overcomers, those who are faithful to Him, will never be condemned, but instead be given a white stone inscribed with a new name, a pure name that signifies their close personal relationship with Him (see Romans 8:1).

It is important to note that when Jesus returns and the saints are clothed with the fine, white linen, this is referring to the fact that God's faithful, even in the midst of moral corruption and wickedness, by the aid of the Holy Spirit, have Christ's character perfected in them. Furthermore, God's character will be vindicated through His people, thus disproving Satan's lies and accusations that no one on earth could keep the righteous requirements of God's holy law.

Please take note that I'm not trying to say or teach that we will continue living in sin until Jesus returns and then have His character instantaneously perfected in us. By God's grace and the help of the Holy Spirit, we *must* now, at this present time, allow Christ's character to be perfected in us, or there is no way possible that we will be able to stand in the time of Jacob's trouble—in the sight of a holy and just God without a Mediator. If we fail to have Christ's character perfected in us *now*, then we have no one to blame but ourselves if we end up being lost and burning in the lake of fire.

"Some men's sins are open beforehand, going before to judgment; and some *men* they follow after" (1 Timothy 5:24).

"He that covereth his sins shall not prosper: but whoso confesseth and forsaketh *them* shall have mercy" (Proverbs 28:13).

Chapter 4—Quotes on Fine Linen by Ellen G. White

*Please note that the next several passages are quotes from the pen of inspiration and not the original thoughts of the author of this book.

When the king came in to view the guests, the real character of all was revealed. For every guest at the feast there had been provided a wedding garment. This garment was a gift from the king. By wearing it the guests showed their respect for the giver of the feast. But one man was clothed in his common citizen dress. He had refused to make the preparation required by the king. The garment provided for him at great cost he disdained to wear. Thus he insulted his lord. To the king's demand, "How camest thou in hither not having a wedding garment?" he could answer nothing. He was self-condemned. Then the king said, "Bind him hand and foot, and take him away, and cast him into outer darkness."

By the king's examination of the guests at the feast is represented a work of judgment. The guests at the gospel feast are those who profess to serve God, those whose names are written in the book of life. But not all who profess to be Christians are true disciples. Before the final reward is given, it must be decided who are fitted to share the inheritance of the righteous. **This decision must be made prior to the second coming of Christ in the clouds of heaven; for when He comes, His reward is with Him, "to give every man according as his work shall be." Revelation 22:12.** Before His coming, then, the character of every man's work will have been determined, and to every one of Christ's followers the reward will have been apportioned according to his deeds.

It is while men are still dwelling upon the earth that the work of investigative judgment takes place in the courts of heaven. The lives of all His professed followers pass in review before God. All are examined according to the record of the books of heaven, and according to his deeds the destiny of each is forever fixed.

By the wedding garment in the parable is represented the pure, spotless character which Christ's true followers will possess. To the church it is given **"that she should be arrayed in fine linen, clean and white," "not having spot, or wrinkle, or any such thing."**

Revelation 19:8; Ephesians 5:27. The fine linen, says the Scripture, "is the righteousness of saints." Revelation 19:8. It is the righteousness of Christ, His own unblemished character, that through faith is imparted to all who receive Him as their personal Saviour.

The truth is to be planted in the heart. It is to control the mind and regulate the affections. The whole character must be stamped with the divine utterances. Every jot and tittle of the word of God is to be brought into the daily practice.

He who becomes a partaker of the divine nature will be in harmony with God's great standard of righteousness, His holy law. This is the rule by which God measures the actions of men. This will be the test of character in the judgment. (White, *Christ's Object Lessons*, pp. 309–314, emphasis added)

And to her was granted that she should be arrayed in fine linen, clean and white: for the fine linen is the righteousness of saints. **Revelation 19:8.**

The parable of the wedding garment [**Matthew 22:1–14**] opens before us a lesson of the highest consequence. ... By the wedding garment in the parable is represented the pure, spotless character which Christ's true followers will possess. ... The fine linen, says the Scripture, "is the righteousness of saints." It is the righteousness of Christ, His own unblemished character, that through faith is imparted to all who receive Him as their personal Saviour.

We cannot provide a robe of righteousness for ourselves, for the prophet says, **"All our righteousness are as filthy rags"** (**Isaiah 64:6**). There is nothing in us from which we can clothe the soul so that its nakedness shall not appear. We are to receive the robe of righteousness woven in the loom of heaven, even the spotless robe of Christ's righteousness. (**White,** *God's Amazing Grace***, p. 24)**

Ample provisions have been made for all who sincerely, earnestly, and thoughtfully set about the work of perfecting holiness in the fear of God. Strength, grace, and glory have been provided through Christ, to be brought by ministering angels to the heirs of salvation. None are so low, so corrupt and vile, that they cannot find in Jesus, who died for them, strength, purity, and righteousness, if they will put away their sins, cease their course of iniquity, and turn with full purpose of heart to the living God. He is waiting to strip them of their garments, stained and polluted by sin, and to put upon them the white, bright robes of righteousness; and He bids them live and not die. In Him they may flourish. Their branches will not wither nor be fruitless. If they abide in Him, they can draw sap and nourishment from Him, be imbued with His Spirit, walk even as He walked, overcome as He overcame, and be exalted to His own right hand. **(White,** *Our Father Cares***, p. 320)**

Chapter 5—Further Discussion on Colors and Coverings

The following is a summary of the four colors that were used in the curtains and their threadings, as well as what they represent and how they point us to Jesus' earthly ministry and purpose in coming to our sin-laden world. The materials used for the first of the four coverings of the sanctuary were blue, purple, and scarlet thread and fine-woven linen. It was made in such a way that the four colors would be visible from inside the sanctuary. Artistic designs of angels were also woven into it so that they would look down at the sanctuary from above, thus bringing back to our remembrance what the apostle Paul told us: **"Are they not all ministering spirits, sent forth to minister for them who shall be heirs of salvation?" (Hebrews 1:14).**

The spiritual meaning of each of these four threads is fascinating. He came to this earth as the representative of mankind, was baptized by John the Baptist, and bore all the sins of the world, just as the sacrificial offerings of the Old Testament had accepted the iniquities of sinners passed onto them through the laying on of hands. Jesus washed away all the sins of the world by bearing the condemnation of these sins all at once.

The purple thread, on the other hand, tells us that Jesus Christ, who came to this earth, is the King of kings and God manifest in the flesh **(i.e., our fallen, sinful nature)**. He is God Himself in His essence. The scarlet thread exhibited in the sanctuary tells us that Jesus, having at once accepted all our sins, shed His blood on the cross and thereby bore the sacrifice and condemnation of our sins in our stead.

The baptism of Jesus and His death on the cross reflected the sacrificial system of the Old Testament, where unblemished offerings accepted the iniquities of sinners through the laying on of hands and bled to death to bear the condemnation of these sins. Like this, in the New Testament, Jesus was baptized, went to the cross, shed His blood, and died. The Bible refers to Him as the sacrificial offering.

The name "Jesus" means He "shall save his people from their sins" (Matthew 1:21), and the name "Christ" means "the anointed One." In the Old Testament, three kinds of persons were to be anointed: kings, prophets, and priests. Therefore, the name "Jesus Christ" signifies that He is the Savior, God Himself, High Priest of the kingdom of heaven, and the

Lord of everlasting truth. By coming to this earth, being baptized by John, and shedding His blood for our sins on the cross, He has become our true Lord and Savior.

The first covering of the sanctuary reveals that the Messiah would come through the blue, purple, and scarlet thread and fine-woven linen and thereby save all those who believe in Him from their sins and condemnation. These ministries are none other than the baptism of Jesus and His death on the cross. The mystery of salvation manifested in this four-colored first covering is that the Messiah came to this earth, took upon the sins of mankind by being baptized and crucified, then rose from the dead.

With these ministries, Jesus Christ desires to save those who believe in Him from their sins and make them God's people. He is the King of kings and the sacrificial offering that has blotted out the iniquities of sinners and delivered those who believe in Him and accept Him as their Lord and Savior from their sins and condemnation.

The four coverings of the sanctuary tell us how God has delivered us from our sins in detail. The Messiah would come to this earth in the our fallen human nature, take upon Himself all the sins of the world, be crucified for the punishment thereof, remit (**cancel or refrain from exacting or inflicting a debt or punishment**) the guilty record of His people, and save them from their iniquity with His own blood. However, this salvation is fulfilled only in those who believe in the Messiah as their Savior. We must all believe that Jesus Christ, as manifested in the materials of the coverings of the sanctuary, indeed came by His baptism and death on the cross and has thereby saved us once for all from our sins.

In accordance with the colors of blue, purple, and scarlet thread manifested in the coverings of the sanctuary, the Son of God came to us as the sacrificial offering of the New Testament time, was baptized, and shed His blood on the cross. Moreover, by believing in the Messiah revealed in the coverings of the sanctuary, we can give God the offering of faith that saves us.

As such, we must believe in the truth manifested in the blue, purple, and scarlet thread. If anyone does not come before God and thus fails to give the offering of faith by believing in the ministries of Jesus manifested in the blue, purple, and scarlet thread, they will surely pay the penalty for their sins with their own lives. However, if one believes in this truth, then by faith accepts the gift of salvation freely offered through our Lord Jesus, that person can go before God at all times as His child. The sanctuary shows us that those who do not believe in Jesus Christ, who became the sacrificial offering and was manifested in the blue, purple, and scarlet thread, can never enter the kingdom of God.

The sanctuary's coverings, as well as the rest of its materials and furnishings, thus show us the way to heaven. We must find the way to enter the kingdom of heaven by believing in the truth revealed in the sanctuary service and blue, purple, and scarlet thread. Those who want to enter the kingdom of God must first have their problem of sin resolved by believing in the truth of the remission of sin manifested in the blue, purple, and scarlet thread. As such, whether people enter into His church by believing in this truth or are rejected by Him for not believing is a choice that they must make.

> *The sanctuary's coverings, as well as the rest of its materials and furnishings, thus show us the way to heaven.*

Of course, our consciences are at liberty to believe or not believe that the sanctuary reveals to us the whole plan of salvation and restitution of all things through our Lord Jesus. However, you should also recognize that the result of not believing in this truth will be too catastrophic for anyone to endure. For us to enter the kingdom of God according to His will, we must be forever saved from our sins by believing in the Messiah and accepting His death on the cross. All must accept and believe in their hearts that the death of the Messiah on the cross has remitted all their sins. Only when they believe can they receive the everlasting remission of unrighteousness and enter into the glory of God.

Chapter 6—What Does Goat's Hair Represent In the Bible?

In this section of our study, we are going to discover the purpose of the goats' hair, rams' skins dyed red, badgers' (seals') skins, and shittim (acacia) wood. The material used for the second covering of the tabernacle was goats' hair. This tells us that the Messiah to come would justify mankind by delivering them from their sins and the condemnation thereof. In other words, for human beings to receive the righteousness of God, it is necessary for them to believe in the gospel of the water, blood, and Spirit. The righteousness of God has washed our hearts as white as snow and thereby enabled us to receive the remission of our sins.

Goats' Hair (Cursed Sin Offering)

Goats were commonly used in those days for their milk, meat, skin (for things such as water bottles), and hair, which was very long, dark, and coarse and spun and woven into cloth. The goat was a sacrificial animal. The **goats' hair** covering was the first above the tabernacle curtain. This drab color tells us of Jesus in His humility and poverty.

Goatskins were worn by the poor and, throughout the Bible, represented extreme poverty. *"They were stoned, they were sawn in two, were tempted, were slain with the sword. They wandered about in sheepskins and goatskins, being destitute, afflicted, tormented" (Heb. 11:37, NKJV).* *"And Jesus said to him, 'Foxes have holes and birds of the air **have nests, but the Son of Man has nowhere to lay His head'" (Luke 9:58, NKJV).*** The hair speaks of Christ as the separated One. Just as the hair must be separated from the goat, so Christ had to sacrifice His own covering to provide a covering for others.

Another interesting point about the goat is that it was used on the Day of Atonement. During this time of investigation, there were two goats brought to the sanctuary. One was the Lord's goat, which represented Jesus; the other was the scapegoat, which represented Satan. After the high priest completed the blood sprinkling in the Holy of Holies, he would go into the court of the tabernacle and lay his hands on the head of the scapegoat, confessing over it all the sins of the people. The goat was then led away by a man standing ready into the wilderness and left in isolation to signify the carrying away of Israel's sins, which God had forgiven.

This reminds us that there is coming a time in the not-too-distant future when God will blot out all the iniquities of His faithful people. Just as the scapegoat was led away into the wilderness to bear the sins of the children of Israel, so Satan, the originator of sin, will bear the punishment for our sins that are blotted out of the record books in heaven. He will incur the penalty of them in the lake of fire at the end of the thousand-year reign of the saints in heaven with Jesus, ultimately to be destroyed and never to tempt, annoy, or harass the redeemed to sin ever again!

"For He made Him who knew no sin to be sin for us, that we might become the righteousness of God in Him" (2 Corinthians 5:21, NKJV).

Chapter 7—What Do Rams' Skins Dyed Red Represent In the Bible?

The materials used for the third covering of the tabernacle were rams' skins dyed red. This indicates that the Messiah would come to this earth, take upon Himself the sins of the world by being baptized and crucified, and thereby become the sacrificial offering for the iniquity of His people. The blood that Jesus Christ shed on the cross paid the wages of death for the sins of the world. In other words, it tells us that He became the sacrificial offering and saved His people from their sins (see Leviticus 16).

> *The blood that Jesus Christ shed on the cross paid the wages of death for the sins of the world.*

On the Day of Atonement, two goats were prepared to take upon themselves the entire sins of the people of Israel. One of them, the Lord's goat, was a sacrificial offering of atonement that was given to God. As stated in the previous paragraph, this goat represented Jesus and pointed forward to when He would offer Himself up for our sins. At that time, the high priest laid his hands on the head of this first, sacrificial goat, passing all the sins of the people onto it at once. He then took its blood and sprinkled it on the east side of the mercy seat and seven times before the mercy seat. This is how the offering of the atonement of the people of Israel was given to God.

Then, before the witness of the Hebrews gathered around the tabernacle, the high priest put his hands on the scapegoat and passed a year's worth of the sins of the people of Israel. This was to give all of them the conviction that all their sins of the past year were thus taken away from them through the laying on of the high priest's hands. This scapegoat was then sent out to the wilderness to its death, carrying with it all their sins (see **Leviticus 16:21, 22**).

Rams' Skins Dyed Red (Substitutionary Sacrifice)

A ram is a grown, male **sheep** and the head of the flock. A shepherd may have one or two rams in a flock of ewes to promote uniformity. It is forever, in the eyes of the Jew, the substitute animal, faithful unto death. This is, of course, because God provided a ram as a substitute for Isaac on the day when Abraham's faith was revealed.

> *And He said, "Do not lay your hand on the lad, or do anything to him; for now I know that you fear God, since you have not withheld your son, your only son, from Me." Then Abraham lifted his eyes and looked, and there behind him was a ram caught in a thicket by its* **horns***. So Abraham went and took the ram, and offered it up for a* **burnt offering** *instead of his son. (Genesis 22:12, 13, NKJV)*

Rams' skins were **dyed red** to represent the sacrifice of a substitute, so Jesus, as the head of the human race, the second Adam, sacrificed His own life as a substitute for all who would put their trust in Him.

> *But we see Jesus, who was made a little lower than the angels, for the suffering of death crowned with glory and honor, that He, by the grace of God, might taste death for everyone. … Therefore, in all things He had to be made like* His *brethren, that He might be a merciful and faithful High Priest in things* pertaining *to God, to make propitiation for the sins of the people. (Hebrews 2:9, 17)*
>
> *"The next day John saw Jesus coming toward him, and said, "Behold! The Lamb of God who takes away the sin of the world!" (John 1:29, NKJV)*

Chapter 8—What Do Badgers' Skins Represent In the Bible?

Outward Appearance—Unattractive

Badgers' skins were the final, outer covering that everyone saw. They were tough, coarse, and very plain in their appearance, but how does this speak of Christ? It speaks of what He was to humanity. There was no outward beauty to the tabernacle proper; so it was with Christ when He came to earth and pitched His tabernacle among mankind. As the prophet foretold, *"Who has believed our report? And to whom has the arm of the LORD been revealed? For He shall grow up before Him as a tender plant, and as a root out of dry ground. He has no form or comeliness; And when we see Him,* There is *no beauty that we should desire Him" (Isaiah 53:1, 2, NKJV).*

What was Jesus to the Jews? Nothing but a coarse, hard badger skin. What is Jesus to the world today? Nothing but a coarse, hard badger skin. However, to those of us who have opened our hearts to Him, He is much, much more. He is the "altogether lovely One," "Rose of Sharon," "Lily of the Valley," and "fairest among 10,000" to our souls. If anyone desired to look beyond the outer flesh covering, that person would see the transfiguration of Christ's glory. "Can any good thing come out of Nazareth?"

> *He was in the world, and the world was made through Him, and the world did not know Him. He came to His own, and His own did not receive Him. But as many as received Him, to them He gave the right to become children of God, to those who believe in His name: who were born, not of blood, nor of the will of the flesh, nor of the will of man, but of God. And the Word became flesh and dwelt among us, and we beheld His glory, the glory as of the only begotten of the Father, full of grace and truth. (John 1:10–14, NKJV)*

Badgers' skins reflect our image, as well as the image of the Lord when He came to this earth. He came to this earth in the flesh of a man to call sinners to repentance and make them righteous. Badgers' skins also tell us that Jesus Christ did not raise Himself high when He came to this earth, but instead lowered Himself as a man of humble birth.

Chapter 9—What Does Acacia Wood Symbolize In the Bible?

Please open your Bibles to Exodus 25. In our study of the tabernacle, we have examined the pattern as it was given to Moses and the construction as it was followed by Bezaleel. Therefore, we have two descriptions of the tabernacle. There are details in each that supplement the other, and the only way we can have a full picture is to notice the two accounts at the right times. There may not always be a need, but when there is, we will observe two pertinent sections of Scripture. The first is Exodus 25–31 and the other is 35–40.

> **And the LORD SPAKE UNTO MOSES, SAYING, Speak unto the children of Israel, that they bring me an offering: of every man that giveth it willingly with his heart ye shall take my offering. And this *is* the offering which ye shall take of them; gold, and silver, and brass, And blue, and purple, and scarlet, and fine linen, and goats'** *hair,* **And rams' skins dyed red, and badgers' skins, and shittim wood, Oil for the light, spices for anointing oil, and for sweet incense, Onyx stones, and stones to be set in the ephod, and in the breastplate. And let them make me a sanctuary; that I may dwell among them. According to all that I shew thee,** *after* **the pattern of the tabernacle, and the pattern of all the instruments thereof, even so shall ye make** *it.* **(Exodus 25:1–9)**

This passage describes for us a stockpile of material from which the tabernacle and its furnishings were to be made. We are interested in two kinds of materials that were taken from this list to build the piece of furniture that we will soon be considering. We are interested in the gold of verse 3 and shittim wood of verse 5 because these are the two materials from which the ark of the covenant was made. It was the piece of furniture found in the Most Holy Place. It was a chest-like object with four rings, one at each corner, staves through the rings for conveyance, and two cherubim on top looking down on the mercy seat, which was the lid of the ark.

We have found that the purpose of the ark was the sustenance of life. We noticed how the word "ark" is used in the Bible: Noah's ark, the ark in which Moses was placed when his mother was saving his life from Pharaoh, and the ark of the covenant. The latter followed the example of the other two in the sustenance of life.

We found that especially true when we noticed its contents. There were the two tables of stone that had inscribed upon them the Ten Commandments, the disobedience of which would have resulted in death if they had not been covered by the mercy seat. There was the golden pot of manna that spoke of the bread by which the people were able to live. There was Aaron's rod that budded, which spoke of the intercessory work of the Savior.

Now we want to look at the ark of the covenant itself, remembering that it symbolizes the Lord Jesus Christ. As we look at the ark, I trust that we will be able to see that more definitely. We have looked at the stockpile of material in Exodus 25:1–9 and are especially interested in the gold of verse 3 and shittim wood of verse 5. If you look at the following passage, you will see how Bezaleel, the architect of the tabernacle, took these two materials and constructed from them the ark of the covenant:

> And they shall make an ark of shittim wood: two cubits and a half shall be the length thereof, and a cubit and a half the breadth thereof, and a cubit and a half the height thereof. And thou shalt overlay it with pure gold, within and without shalt thou overlay it, and shalt make upon it a crown of gold round about. And thou shalt cast four rings of gold for it, and put them in the four corners thereof; and two rings shall be in the one side of it, and two rings in the other side of it. And thou shalt make staves of shittim wood, and overlay them with gold. And thou shalt put the staves into the rings by the sides of the ark, that the ark may be borne with them. The staves shall be in the rings of the ark: they shall not be taken from it. And thou shalt put into the ark the testimony which I shall give thee. (Exodus 25:10–16)

These verses describe how Bezaleel made the ark of the covenant from these specific materials. Let's glance at verse 10 to remind ourselves that the ark was made of shittim wood, as were the staves by which the ark was carried (see v. 13). The word "shittim" is not a translation, but a transliteration—a foreign word spelled with equivalent English letters. Actually, this is the Hebrew word *shittah*.

People were nonplused for a long time regarding what shittim wood was. Then they began to examine the vegetation of the Bible, which is a very intriguing study, and discovered that what we call "shittim" was actually the wood of the acacia tree. The acacia grew in many of the areas that the children of Israel occupied and gave the name to some of the places where they grew.

Location of the Acacia Trees

I would like us to see a specific point, so let's turn our Bibles to Numbers 33, which describes the journeyings of the children of Israel. "And they removed from Almondiblathaim, and pitched in the mountains of Abarim, before Nebo. And they departed from the mountains of Abarim, and pitched in the plains of Moab by Jordan *near* Jericho. And they pitched by Jordan, from Bethjesimoth *even* unto Abelshittim in the plains of Moab" (vs. 47–49).

Notice the name "Abelshittim." This was the name of a place. When people began searching to find out what shittim wood was, they noticed this word transliterated. When they located these places geographically, they were able to arrive at the meaning, for the word "Abel-shittim," which is a definite location on the map, means "the shadow of the shittim tree" or "the meadow of the acacia tree." When they found this place, they saw acacia trees completely surrounding it. Therefore, they realized that the acacia tree was the shittim tree of the Bible. Acacia trees are growing in the same location in the holy land today. They are very similar to a mesquite tree in their shape, leaves, and thorns.

Judges 7 deals with the battle of Israel against the Midianites. The Lord used Gideon and his 300 men to deliver His people from oppression. **"And the three hundred blew the trumpets, and the Lord set every man's sword against his fellow, even throughout all the host: and the host fled to Bethshittah in Zererath,** *and* **to the border of Abelmeholah, unto Tabbath" (Judges 7:22).** Notice the name "Bethshittah." This was the name of a town. The word "beth" means "home" or "house," so it was the "house of Shittah" or the "house of the acacia tree." When this village was located, sure enough, the most prominent tree there was the acacia tree.

"And it shall come to pass in that day, *that* **the mountains shall drop down new wine, and the hills shall flow with milk, and all the rivers of Judah shall flow with waters, and a fountain shall come forth out of the house of the Lord, and shall water the valley of Shittim" (Joel 3:18).** The Valley of Shittim is an actual location. This prophecy refers to the day when the Lord Jesus Christ will return to this earth, and the desert will blossom as the rose. The Valley of Shittim was a very parched area, and shittim trees, or acacia trees, grew in abundance in the wilderness of Sinai because they were specially adapted to dry soil.

Characteristic of the Environment

The reason we have turned to these various passages of Scripture and established the identity of the acacia tree is so we can understand why God chose this particular tree to provide the wood from which the ark of the covenant was made. First, one reason He chose it was that it was characteristic of the Israelites' environment and, from a purely practical standpoint, an easy wood for them to attain. If we stop our comment there, we will miss the spiritual significance entirely. We need to remember that one of the reasons God instructed them to use a tree that was characteristic of their environment was that in so doing, they would provide a spiritual lesson for us.

> *The reason we have turned to these various passages of Scripture and established the identity of the acacia tree is so we can understand why God chose this particular tree to provide the wood from which the ark of the covenant was made.*

The Word of God can express it better than I can, so please see the following verses, which is a testimony to this fact. Hebrews 2 speaks of the witness that God bore regarding salvation for the human race and what He intended before the fall. Paul spoke of mankind, then shifted to the Son of Man, the Lord Jesus Christ:

> But one in a certain place testified, saying, What is man, that thou art mindful of him? or the son of man, that thou visitest him? Thou madest him a little lower than the angels; thou crownedst him with glory and honour, and didst set him over the works of thy hands: Thou hast put all things in subjection under his feet. For in that he put all in subjection under him, he left nothing *that is* not put under him. But now we see not yet all things put under him. (Hebrews 2:6–8)

Chapter 10—An Illustration of Christ's Incarnation

As though the apostle Paul was anticipating an argument from his readers, he said, "Thou hast put all things in subjection under his feet. For in that he put all in subjection under him, he left nothing *that is* not put under him. But now we see not yet all things put under him" (Hebrews 2:8).

When we read this passage, we are apt to say, "Now, wait a minute, Paul! We don't see mankind crowned with glory and honor. We see it crowned with sickness and death. We don't see all things put under humanity. We see it at the mercy of everything and everyone. Someone has made a mistake, didn't you, Paul?"

He answered, "I did not make a mistake. We do not see him that way *yet*."

> But we see Jesus, who was made a little lower than the angels for the suffering of death, crowned with glory and honour; that he by the grace of God should taste death for every man. For it became him, for whom *are* all things, and by whom *are* all things, in bringing many sons unto glory, to make the captain of their salvation perfect through sufferings. For both he that sanctifieth and they who are sanctified *are* all of one: for which cause he is not ashamed to call them brethren, Saying, I will declare thy name unto my brethren, in the midst of the church will I sing praise unto thee. And again, I will put my trust in him. And again, Behold I and the children which God hath given me. Forasmuch then as the children are partakers of flesh and blood, he also himself likewise took part of the same; that through death he might destroy him that had the power of death, that is, the devil; And deliver them who through fear of death were all their lifetime subject to bondage. For verily he took not on *him the nature of* angels; but he took on *him* the seed of Abraham. Wherefore in all things it behooved him to be made like unto *his* brethren, that he might be a merciful and faithful high priest in things *pertaining* to God, to make reconciliation for the sins of the people. For in that he himself hath suffered being tempted, he is able to succor them that are tempted. (Hebrews 2:9–18)

You will see in Hebrews 2—Paul's discussion of the incarnation of the Lord Jesus Christ—the reason the acacia tree was chosen by God as characteristic of the environment in which the children of Israel lived. It illustrated the fact that when Christ became the sacrifice for the sins of the world, He had to become exactly like the people for whom He died. Had He not done so, salvation would not have been effectual.

He did not take upon Himself the nature of angels, but mankind. **"But Jesus accepted humanity when the race had been weakened by four thousand years of sin" (White 1898, p. 49)**. That is why we are encouraged to pray, take our burdens to the Lord, and leave them there (see Hebrews 2:18 above).

Our finite minds cannot comprehend this great truth, but the Bible very plainly tells us that the Lord Jesus Christ suffered everything that we have ever suffered. He knows what we are suffering now. One may ask, "He never broke a leg. How does He know that hurts?" I cannot explain it, but the Bible says He can empathize. One might ask, "Well, He was never married. He never lost a wife. What does He know about that?" I cannot explain it, but the Bible says that He was tested on all points like we are. He knows every heartache and longing that we have.

> *Our finite minds cannot comprehend this great truth, but the Bible very plainly tells us that the Lord Jesus Christ suffered everything that we have ever suffered. He knows what we are suffering now.*

That should be a great blessing to our hearts. We try to comfort one another, but we may as well face the fact that the best we can do is to say, "I sympathize with you." If we have never gone through that particular trial, we do not know what it is, in spite of what we may say. The acacia tree, peculiar to the environment in which they existed, illustrates the great truth that the Lord Jesus Christ took upon Himself, not the nature of the angels or the unfallen nature of Adam, but the fallen nature of humanity.

Shade in a Dry Land

I would like you to notice some of the characteristics of the acacia tree because I believe that there is another reason the Lord chose it as the material for the ark. One of the characteristics of the acacia wood, as we deduced from Joel 3:18, is that it flourished in dry places. It is peculiar to the desert. It will grow when nothing else will. It is not particularly attractive or beautiful, but it provides **shade** in a dry and thirsty land.

Isaiah presented a picture of our Lord Jesus Christ. In my mind, this is one of the most beautiful depictions of the Savior in all the Bible. It becomes even more effective if you change the plural pronoun to the singular pronoun and let it speak to your own heart: "Who hath believed our report? and to whom is the arm of the LORD revealed? For he shall grow up before him as a tender plant, and as a root out of a dry ground: he hath no form nor comeliness; and when we shall see him, *there is* no beauty that we should desire him" (Isaiah 53:1, 2). Isaiah anticipated the reaction of the people who would see Jesus when He came to the earth.

Chapter 11—The Finished Work

He is despised and rejected of men; a man of sorrows, and acquainted with grief: and we hid as it were *our* faces from him; he was despised, and we esteemed him not. Surely he hath borne our griefs, and carried our sorrows: yet we did esteem him stricken, smitten of God, and afflicted. But he *was* wounded for our transgressions, *he was* bruised for our iniquities: the chastisement of our peace *was* upon him; and with his stripes we are healed. All we like sheep have gone astray; we have turned every one to his own way; and the LORD hath laid on him the iniquity of us all. He was oppressed, and he was afflicted, yet he opened not his mouth: he is brought as a lamb to the slaughter, and as a sheep before her shearers is dumb, so he openeth not his mouth. He was taken from prison and from judgment: and who shall declare his generation? for he was cut off out of the land of the living: for the transgression of my people was he stricken. (Isaiah 53:3–8)

Before we leave this passage, let me suggest that you have the answer to the question, "Who is to finish what He came to do?" Jesus came to redeem the world and paid the price in full, but the world will never be redeemed unless we pick up where He left off and tell the story.

And he made his grave with the wicked [a prophecy of the crucifixion between two thieves], and with the rich in his death [a prophecy of His burial in the sepulcher of Joseph of Arimathaea]; because he had done no violence, neither *was any* deceit in his mouth. Yet it pleased the LORD to bruise him; he hath put *him* to grief: when thou shalt make his soul an offering for sin, he shall see *his* seed, he shall prolong *his* days, and the pleasure of the LORD shall prosper in his hand. (Isaiah 53:9, 10)

Get the picture: Jehovah bruised Him even though there was nothing in Him that merited the bruising. Have you ever wondered whether it ever crossed the mind of the Savior, 'Was it worth it? Was it worth giving My life? Was it worth all the suffering I endured?' Well, the answer is that when he sees those who come into a saving knowledge of Him being born again, He is satisfied.

He shall see of the travail of his soul, *and* shall be satisfied: by his knowledge shall my righteous servant justify many; for he shall bear their iniquities. Therefore will I divide him *a portion* with the great, and he shall divide the spoil with the strong; because he hath poured out his soul unto death: and he was numbered with the transgressors; and he bare the sin of many, and made intercession for the transgressors. (Isaiah 53:11, 12)

Let Isaiah 53 be a blessing to your heart again and again. It can be. It won't be if you are filled with your own righteousness. It won't be if you are not conscious of your unworthiness. However, if you are aware of your sinfulness, this chapter can be a great blessing to you.

Go back to verse 2 because it is why we read the chapter. When Isaiah, by the Holy Spirit, prophesied the kind of person the Lord Jesus would be, he said He would be as a root out of the dry ground. If you wanted to illustrate that with wood, would it not be wise to select a wood that had that very characteristic? That is what our God did when He chose the acacia tree for the ark of the covenant.

The Incorruptible Word of God

Let us think of another characteristic of acacia wood. Did you know that for all practical purposes, it is indestructible? Trees in that area of the world were often destroyed by worms that bored from within and caused them to die and rendered the wood useless, but the acacia tree had the unusual characteristic of being impervious to these worms. It was indestructible and incorruptible. When we think about that, we are reminded of what we read about another trait of the Savior. "Being born again, not of corruptible seed, but of incorruptible, by the word of God, which liveth and abideth forever" (1 Peter 1:23).

Did you notice that phrase? The incorruptible Word of God is the written Word, but we must not forget that it is the living Word as well. We are reminded, "In the beginning was the Word, and the Word was with God, and the Word was God" (John 1:1).

When seventy Greek scholars translated the Old Testament from Hebrew into Greek, they produced the version of the Bible to which we refer as the Septuagint. The Greek word that they selected to describe the wood from which the ark was made is translated "incorruptible" here. Indeed, we are not too far afield when we suggest that the acacia wood was chosen as the material for the ark because it symbolizes the incorruptible Word of God.

Thorns Illustrate Suffering

If you want a good illustration of the acacia tree, you may look at a mesquite tree. It is shaped somewhat the same, the leaves are somewhat the same, and the characteristic thorns are there. As we teach symbolism, I dare not pass over that lightly. I think there was a reason why God chose a tree with thorns.

Exodus 25 mentions a crown of gold, but that was not the only crown the Savior wore. In the verses below, read of another crown He wore—a crown of thorns, plaited from wood very similar to this. Thus, in the acacia tree, there is another illustration of our Lord and His coming to earth. It speaks not only of indestructibility but also the suffering He endured when He wore that crown of thorns.

> Then Pilate therefore took Jesus, and scourged *him*. And the soldiers platted a crown of thorns, and put *it* on his head, and they put on him a purple robe, And said, Hail, King of the Jews! And they smote him with their hands. Pilate therefore went forth again, and saith unto them, Behold, I bring him forth to you, that ye may know that I find no fault in him. Then came Jesus forth, wearing the crown of thorns, and the purple robe. And *Pilate* saith unto them, Behold the man! (John 19:1–5)

Pierced for Healing

Right along that line, I would suggest a fourth characteristic of the acacia tree. It had within it sap that would flow only when the tree was pierced at night. The gum that came forth from the pierced acacia tree was used for medicinal purposes. Here again, we have another illustration that we dare not pass over lightly, particularly when we call to mind what we just read in Isaiah 53.

We read that He was wounded for our transgressions, bruised for our iniquities, the chastisement of our peace was upon Him, and with His stripes, we are healed. Notice the words "wounded," "bruised," "chastisement," and "stripes." They are all summed up in the word—"piercing." Did you see the result of it? We are healed. Just as the acacia tree was pierced at nightfall, and the sap flowed to provide medicine for the healing of the human body, our Savior, the Lord Jesus Christ, was pierced in those dark hours on Calvary, and that piercing resulted in something far

> *Just as the acacia tree was pierced at nightfall, and the sap flowed to provide medicine for the healing of the human body, our Savior, the Lord Jesus Christ, was pierced in those dark hours on Calvary, and that piercing resulted in something far more important than physical health. It resulted in spiritual health and eternal life.*

more important than physical health. It resulted in spiritual health and eternal life.

Deity Limited by Flesh

"And they shall make an ark *of* shittim wood: two cubits and a half *shall be* the length thereof, and a cubit and a half the breadth thereof, and a cubit and a half the height thereof" (Exodus 25:10). Immediately after we are told that the ark was made of shittim wood, we are given its dimensions and informed that it had to be made precisely according to those dimensions. In our introductory study of the sanctuary, we repeatedly found the emphasis that Bezaleel must not deviate even a hair's breadth from the pattern that was given to Moses in the mount.

In verse 10, you will notice that the dimensions of the ark were restricted. They were to be two cubits and a half, a cubit and a half, and a cubit and a half. It was not a matter of making a big chest or a small one. It was a matter of limiting the chest to specific dimensions. This is one of the best illustrations of what the incarnation means. It means that deity is limited by the flesh.

The passage below provides a very concrete illustration of how the Lord Jesus Christ limited His deity. This is a thrilling passage of Scripture, and every time I read it, I wish I might have been there in the bushes, observing what was going on, because it was an exhilarating and exciting thing:

> When Jesus had spoken these words, he went forth with his disciples over the brook Cedron, where was a garden, into the which he entered, and his disciples. And Judas also, which betrayed him, knew the place: for Jesus ofttimes resorted thither with his disciples. Judas then, having received a band *of men* and officers

from the chief priests and Pharisees, cometh thither with lanterns and torches and weapons. Jesus therefore, knowing all things that should come upon him, went forth, and said unto them, Whom seek ye? They answered him, Jesus of Nazareth. Jesus saith unto them, I am *he*. And Judas also, which betrayed him, stood with them. As soon then as he had said unto them, I am *he*, they went backward, and fell to the ground. Then asked he them again, Whom seek ye? And they said, Jesus of Nazareth. Jesus answered, I have told you that I am *he*: if therefore ye seek me, let these go their way: That the saying might be fulfilled, which he spake, Of them which thou gavest me have I lost none. Then Simon Peter having a sword drew it, and smote the high priest's servant, and cut off his right ear. The servant's name was Malchus. Then said Jesus unto Peter, Put up thy sword into the sheath: the cup which my Father hath given me, shall I not drink it? Then the band and the captain and officers of the Jews took Jesus, and bound him, And led him away to Annas first; for he was father in law to Caiaphas, which was the high priest that same year. Now Caiaphas was he, which gave counsel to the Jews, that it was expedient that one man should die for the people. (John 18:1–14)

I hope you will get the feel of this passage. The Lord Jesus came into the Garden of Gethsemane from the upper room. He knew what was going to happen. Judas and the men who were with him, carrying lanterns and swords, approached Christ, and He asked, "For whom are you looking?"

They answered, "Jesus of Nazareth."

Jesus said, "I am He." Did you notice what happened immediately after that? They went backward and fell to the ground. Why do you suppose they did that? If you examine the story carefully, you will see why. The deity of the Lord was permitted to shine through His humanity. When they stood in the presence of the glory of God, they fell on the ground as though they were dead. People cannot stand in the divine presence.

They arose to their feet, and He asked, "Whom are you looking for?"

They replied, "Jesus of Nazareth."

He said, "I am He. You don't need these other fellows. Let them go." Did you notice what the Scripture said? They took Him. Is that a contradiction? Did two different people write the story? Not at all. I believe the Spirit of God inspired the recording of this account to remind us that while He was on the earth, the Lord Jesus Christ willingly limited His deity. He did not have to do so.

Matthew 26 records this same incident and tells how Peter took his sword and cut off the ear of the servant of the high priest. Peter's aim was poor. He did not aim for his ear; he aimed for his head. Did you notice what Jesus said to him?

"Peter, put your sword away. I don't need it. Don't you know that all I would have to is lift one finger toward heaven, and My armies that are waiting there would come swooping through the sky, and these people would be helpless in their presence?" Why did He not do that? He limited His deity in relation to His humanity, just as the ark of the covenant was restricted to a particular size. I believe that is the reason for it.

Chapter 12—A Partial Picture of Jesus

Please turn back with me to Exodus 25, notice the size of this chest again, and recognize that the figure that is emphasized more than any other is one-half. The word "half" in Hebrew is elsewhere translated "part." Why was it that "half" was repeated in the dimensions of the ark of the covenant? I believe that it was meant to tell us a story. Remember what is recorded in 1 Kings 10:6–7. The Queen of Sheba came to see Solomon. Keep in mind that Solomon is an Old Testament type of the Lord Jesus Christ. The queen essentially said, "I have heard of you. But the half [this is the same word used in Exodus 25] has not yet been told me."

I think the apostle Paul had this same thing in mind when he said, "For now we see through a glass, darkly; but then face to face: now I know in part; but then shall I know even as also I am known" (1 Corinthians 13:12). I believe that this half figure is emphasized in the ark to remind us that it—a picture of the deity and humanity of the Lord Jesus Christ—was but a partial picture of the Son of God.

Remember what John said in his first epistle: "Beloved, now are we the sons of God, and it doth not yet appear what we shall be: but we know that, when he shall appear, we shall be like him; for we shall see him as he is" (3:2). We know only in part right now.

When we see the Lord Jesus Christ upon the earth and read His story of redemption and what He can do for humanity now, we see only half the story of the grace of God. Read Ephesians 1, and you will realize that you will not read the other half of the story of His grace until we are with Him in glory.

Three is the number of manifestation. That is why three is the number of the Godhead. God the Father, God the Son, and God the Holy Spirit are a full manifestation of the Godhead. You do not have a manifestation of the Godhead unless you have all three members. Half of three is one and one-half. Here is the same truth emphasized again. The Lord Jesus Christ, as we see His humanity and His deity intertwined and combined, is but half the revelation of God. Someday, when we stand in His presence and the kingdoms of the world become His kingdom, we will have the full manifestation of God in all His glory.

Gold Depicts Divinity

"And thou shalt overlay it with pure gold, within and without shalt thou overlay it, and shalt make upon it a crown of gold round about" (Exodus 25:11). Gold is the second material in our stockpile. It overlaid the ark of the covenant, within and without, and the staves by which it was carried. What is the significance of gold? The way to determine the symbolism of a type in the Bible is to notice the first place in which it is used, and it will typically be used the same way.

Gold is first mentioned in Genesis 2:11–12. It is a thing of great value. The next time we find it mentioned symbolically is in Job 23:10, and there we find that it is more valuable than anything else on this planet. It is above and beyond any earthly thing. In Revelation 21:18, we see the consummation of our journey through the Bible. Gold comes to stand for deity and the glory of the divine.

As you glance back at Exodus 25:11, you will find that the wood of the acacia tree, which stood for the humanity of the Lord Jesus Christ, is overlaid with gold. Humanity is overlaid with deity. The gold overlaid the ark within and without. That is, it was so intertwined that the gold and wood almost became one. You could not talk about one without talking about the other.

"The name of the first *is* Pison: that *is* it which compasseth the whole land of Havilah, where *there is* gold; And the gold of that land *is* good: there *is* bdellium and the onyx stone" (Genesis 2:11, 12).

"But he knoweth the way that I take: *when* he hath tried me, I shall come forth as gold" (Job 23:10).

"And the building of the wall of it was *of* jasper: and the city *was* pure gold, like unto clear glass. (Revelation 21:18).

Humanity and Divinity Intermingled

The Bible does not say this, but I will say it. You do not have to accept it as the Word of God. Josephus, a historian who made a study of the sanctuary and wrote many things about it, said that the gold overlaying the wooden ark was beaten upon it to such an extent that the grain of the wood showed through the gold. It is possible that it is true. If it is, it is very interesting, I think, because it indicates that the humanity of Christ often showed through His divinity and vice versa.

One of the best illustrations of that is found in the story of Jesus on the boat when the storm came. He was asleep in the stern of the ship, probably because He was so tired. The disciples were alarmed and awakened Him out of sleep. **"And he arose, and rebuked the wind, and said unto the sea, Peace, be still. And the wind ceased, and there was a great calm" (Mark 4:39).** "Be quiet" is the literal meaning of the phrase "Peace, be still," just as you would tell a little puppy that was stirring about too much, "Lie down." That is what the Savior said to the waves, and they lay down. Do you see how closely intermingled His humanity and divinity were? They were almost inseparable.

Crowned with Glory and Honor

Glance again at Exodus 25:11 and notice that upon the top of the ark was a crown of gold. That is significant, it seems to me, if you keep in mind where the ark is in the sanctuary. It is in the Most Holy Place, which is typical of the inner chamber of heaven. On the ark that represents the Lord Jesus, we see a crown of gold and are reminded, as we look in the Word of God, that He is to be crowned with glory and honor as no other individual will ever be.

Read Hebrews 2 again. Someone might say, "Wait a minute. Is not our symbolism falling apart here? Is not the ark in the Most Holy Place made of acacia wood? Is that not a sign of humanity? Is the humanity of the Lord Jesus Christ still represented in heaven?" It is. Do you remember what He had in His side, hands, and feet? He has the marks of the nails in His hands and feet and spear in His side. He has them today. He has His glorified body, but the marks of His sojourn on earth are still there. They will be there for us to behold throughout all eternity, so the symbolism does not fall apart. It is still accurate, as all the Word of God is.

Mercy and truth, righteousness and peace, are divine attributes that are wholly made possible by the sacrifice of our Lord Jesus Christ.

"And thou shalt cast four rings of gold for it, and put *them* in the four corners thereof; and two rings *shall be* in the one side of it, and two rings in the other side of it" (Exodus 25:12). These rings were made, not of acacia wood and gold, as were the ark and staves, but of pure gold. I wonder why. Read Psalm 85, which is a salvation song, and notice how the finished work of the Savior is described: "Mercy and truth are met together; righteousness and peace have kissed *each other*" (Psalm 85:10).

Mercy and truth, righteousness and peace, are divine attributes that are wholly made possible by the sacrifice of our Lord Jesus Christ. Notice the rings on the corners of the ark. Between them was the mercy seat, which made possible the combination of these attributes.

An Eternal Memorial

There is one last thing I have to present to you here. That is what is said about the staves: "And thou shalt make staves *of* shittim wood, and overlay them with gold. And thou shalt put the staves into the rings by the sides of the ark, that the ark may be borne with them. The staves shall be in the rings of the ark: they shall not be taken from it" (Exodus 25:13–15).

We know the symbolism: The shittim wood is humanity; the gold is divinity. We are reminded that our Lord Jesus, as a man, bore humanity to God, and as God, bore God to humanity. The two are inseparably related (see v. 15).

While the ark was on the move during the wilderness journeys, the staves were never taken out of those rings. During all the wandering, the ark was needed by traveling people. Read 1 Kings 8, and you will see the "last" journey that the ark made. It remained in Solomon's temple until the time of the Babylonian siege. It was put in the Most Holy Place of the temple, and when the people sang the song of praise, they said, in essence, "God has entered into His rest."

Do you know what they did with those staves? They took them out of the rings of the ark and put them in the corner. It did not need to be carried anymore. Do you know what was left in that ark? Originally, there were Aaron's rod that budded, a golden pot of manna, and the two tables of stone. When it was placed in the temple, its final resting place, the only things left in it were the two tables of stone. Aaron's rod that budded was not there anymore. The golden pot of manna was not there anymore.

I don't think that was an accident. I believe it was God watching over this pattern of timeless truth that He gave us. We no longer need the intercession of Aaron or the manna of the wilderness. However, throughout all eternity, the law of God will be a permanent memorial to the fact that the law "was weak through the flesh," but what it could not do, "God sending His own Son in the likeness of sinful flesh," did (Romans 8:3). The law will be an eternal reminder that we who broke it are saved by Him who fulfilled it.

And the priests brought in the ark of the covenant of the LORD unto his place, into the oracle of the house, to the most holy *place, even* under the wings of the cherubims. For the cherubims spread forth *their* two wings over the place of the ark, and the cherubims covered the ark and the staves thereof above. And they drew out the staves, that the ends of the staves were seen out in the holy *place* before the oracle, and they were not seen without: and there they are unto this day. *There was* nothing in the ark save the two tables of stone, which Moses put there at Horeb, when the LORD made *a covenant* with the children of Israel, when they came out of the land of Egypt. (1 Kings 8:6–9)

And the temple of God was opened in heaven, and there was seen in his temple the ark of his testament. (Revelation 11:19)

For what the law could not do, in that it was weak through the flesh, God sending his own Son in the likeness of sinful flesh, and for sin, condemned sin in the flesh: That the righteousness of the law might be fulfilled in us, who walk not after the flesh, but after the Spirit. (Romans 8:3, 4)

The temple of God was opened in heaven, and there was seen in His temple the ark of His testament." Revelation 11:19. The ark of God's testament is in the holy of holies, the second apartment of the sanctuary. In the ministration of the earthly tabernacle, which served "unto the example and shadow of heavenly things," this apartment was opened only upon the great Day of Atonement for the cleansing of the sanctuary. Therefore the announcement that the temple of God was opened in heaven and the ark of His testament was seen points to the opening of the most holy place of the heavenly sanctuary in 1844 as Christ entered there to perform the closing work of the atonement. Those who by faith followed their great High Priest as He entered upon His ministry in the most holy place, beheld the ark of His testament. As they had studied the subject of the sanctuary they had come to understand the Saviour's change of ministration, and they saw that He was now officiating before the ark of God, pleading His blood in behalf of sinners.

The ark in the tabernacle on earth contained the two tables of stone, upon which were inscribed the precepts of the law of God. The ark was merely a receptacle for the tables of the law, and the presence of these divine precepts gave to it its value and sacredness. When the temple of God was opened in heaven, the ark of

His testament was seen. Within the holy of holies, in the sanctuary in heaven, the divine law is sacredly enshrined--the law that was spoken by God Himself amid the thunders of Sinai and written with His own finger on the tables of stone.

The law of God in the sanctuary in heaven is the great original, of which the precepts inscribed upon the tables of stone and recorded by Moses in the Pentateuch were an unerring transcript. Those who arrived at an understanding of this important point were thus led to see the sacred, unchanging character of the divine law. They saw, as never before, the force of the Saviour's words: "Till heaven and earth pass, one jot or one tittle shall in no wise pass from the law." Matthew 5:18. The law of God, being a revelation of His will, a transcript of His character, must forever endure, "as a faithful witness in heaven." Not one command has been annulled; not a jot or tittle has been changed. Says the psalmist: "Forever, O Lord, Thy word is settled in heaven." "All His commandments are sure. They stand fast for ever and ever." Psalm 119:89; 111:7, 8.

In the very bosom of the Decalogue is the fourth commandment, as it was first proclaimed: "Remember the Sabbath day, to keep it holy. Six days shalt thou labor, and do all thy work: but the seventh day is the Sabbath of the Lord thy God: in it thou shalt not do any work, thou, nor thy son, nor thy daughter, thy manservant, nor thy maidservant, nor thy cattle, nor thy stranger that is within thy gates: for in six days the Lord made heaven and earth, the sea, and all that in them is, and rested the seventh day: wherefore the Lord blessed the Sabbath day, and hallowed it." Exodus 20:8–11. (White, *The Great Controversy*, pp. 433, 434)

Chapter 13—What Does Oil Symbolize In the Bible?

In this section of our study, we are going to discover for what purposes the oil for the light (*menorah*), spices for the anointing oil, and sweet incense were used, and what they symbolize.

What exactly does the oil that was used to keep the *menorah* (golden candlestick) in the Holy Place of the sanctuary represent? To help us find the answer to this question, let us open our Bibles and look at the following texts that deal with this topic:

> And the angel that talked with me came again, and waked me, as a man that is wakened out of his sleep, And said unto me, What seest thou? And I said, I have looked, and behold a candlestick all *of* gold, with a bowl upon the top of it, and his seven lamps thereon, and seven pipes to the seven lamps, which *are* upon the top thereof: And two olive trees by it, one upon the right *side* of the bowl, and the other upon the left *side* thereof. So I answered and spake to the angel that talked with me, saying, What *are* these, my lord? Then the angel that talked with me answered and said unto me, Knowest thou not what these be? And I said, No, my lord. Then he answered and spake unto me, saying, This *is* the word of the LORD unto Zerubbabel, saying, Not by might, nor by power, but by my spirit, saith the LORD of hosts. (Zechariah 4:1–6)

> But ye have an unction from the Holy One, and ye know all things. I have not written unto you because ye know not the truth, but because ye know it, and that no lie is of the truth. (1 John 2:20, 21)

> Then Samuel took the horn of oil, and anointed him in the midst of his brethren: and the Spirit of the LORD came upon David from that day forward. So Samuel rose up, and went to Ramah. (1 Samuel 16:13)

> Until the spirit be poured upon us from on high, and the wilderness be a fruitful field, and the fruitful field be counted for a forest. (Isaiah 32:15)

We have Scriptural authority for seeing the oil as a type of the Holy Spirit. In the Bible, the olive tree is symbolic of many things:

a) Beauty— "His branches shall spread, and his beauty shall be as the olive tree, and his smell as Lebanon" (Hosea 14:6).

b) Fertility—"But I *am* like a green olive tree in the house of God: I trust in the mercy of God for ever and ever" (Psalm 52:8).
c) Richness—"But the olive tree said unto them, Should I leave my fatness, wherewith by me they honour God and man, and go to be promoted over the trees?" (Judges 9:9).

> *The Holy Spirit, represented by olive oil, is the One who possesses all that mankind needs for life and godliness. Richness, fertility, and beauty are all His in an abundant measure.*

The Holy Spirit, represented by olive oil, is the One who possesses all that mankind needs for life and godliness. Richness, fertility, and beauty are all His in an abundant measure. Jesus was anointed by God as a prophet, priest, and king. Everything Christ did was filled with richness, fertility, and beauty because He was the temple of the Holy Spirit and filled with all fullness. For he whom God hath sent speaketh the words of God: for God giveth not the Spirit by measure *unto him*" (John 3:34).

It is interesting that the olives weren't beaten or pressed, but crushed. In like manner, Jesus was crushed in the Garden of Gethsemane (Hebrew for "oil press") and then, by the very wrath of God, on a Roman cross. As the Scriptures say, "Yet it pleased the LORD to bruise him; he hath put *him* to grief: when thou shalt make his soul an offering for sin, he shall see *his* seed, he shall prolong *his* days, and the pleasure of the LORD shall prosper in his hand" (Isaiah 53:10).

The anointing oil was restricted for tabernacle use only. Anyone violating the command was put to death. The olive oil was to be nothing but pure because it represents the Holy Spirit of Christ. The word "Christ" is the Greek equivalent for the Hebrew *"Mashiach"* ("Messiah"), which means "the Anointed One." It literally means "to smear," as with oil. The oil was also used to anoint the holy tabernacle and its furniture and light the golden lampstand.

As Christ sat looking upon the party that waited for the bridegroom, He told His disciples the story of the ten virgins, by their experience illustrating the experience of the church that shall live just before His second coming.

Chapter 13

The two classes of watchers represent the two classes who profess to be waiting for their Lord. They are called virgins because they profess a pure faith. By the lamps is represented the word of God. The psalmist says, "Thy word is a lamp unto my feet, and a light unto may path." Psalm 119:105. The oil is a symbol of the Holy Spirit. Thus the Spirit is represented in the prophecy of Zechariah. "The angel that talked with me came again," he says, "and waked me, as a man that is wakened out of his sleep, and said unto me, What seest thou? And I said, I have looked, and behold a candlestick all of gold, with a bowl upon the top of it, and his seven lamps thereon, and seven pipes to the seven lamps, which are upon the top thereof; and two olive trees by it, one upon the right side of the bowl, and the other upon the left side thereof. So I answered and spake to the angel that talked with me, saying, What are these, my lord? ... Then he answered and spake unto me, saying, This is the word of the Lord unto Zerubbabel, saying, Not by might, nor by power, but by My Spirit, saith the Lord of hosts. ... And I answered again, and said unto him, What be these two olive branches which through the two golden pipes empty the golden oil out of themselves? ... Then said he, These are the two anointed ones, that stand by the Lord of the whole earth." Zechariah 4:1–14.

From the two olive trees the golden oil was emptied through the golden pipes into the bowl of the candlestick, and thence into the golden lamps that gave light to the sanctuary. So from the holy ones that stand in God's presence His Spirit is imparted to the human instrumentalities who are consecrated to His service. The mission of the two anointed ones is to communicate to God's people that heavenly grace which alone can make His word a lamp to the feet and a light to the path. "Not by might, nor by power, but by My Spirit, saith the Lord of hosts." Zechariah 4:6.

In the parable, all the ten virgins went out to meet the bridegroom. All had lamps and vessels for oil. For a time there was seen no difference between them. So with the church that lives just before Christ's second coming. All have a knowledge of the Scriptures. All have heard the message of Christ's near approach, and confidently expect His appearing. But as in the parable, so it is now. A time of waiting intervenes, faith is tried; and when the cry is heard, "Behold, the Bridegroom cometh; go ye out to meet

Him," many are unready. They have no oil in their vessels with their lamps. They are destitute of the Holy Spirit.

Without the Spirit of God a knowledge of His word is of no avail. The theory of truth, unaccompanied by the Holy Spirit, cannot quicken the soul or sanctify the heart. One may be familiar with the commands and promises of the Bible; but unless the Spirit of God sets the truth home, the character will not be transformed. Without the enlightenment of the Spirit, men will not be able to distinguish truth from error, and they will fall under the masterful temptations of Satan. **(White, *Christ's Object Lessons*, pp. 406–411)**

Then shall the kingdom of heaven be likened unto ten virgins, which took their lamps, and went forth to meet the bridegroom. And five of them were wise, and five *were* foolish. They that *were* foolish took their lamps, and took no oil with them: But the wise took oil in their vessels with their lamps. While the bridegroom tarried, they all slumbered and slept. And at midnight there was a cry made, Behold, the bridegroom cometh; go ye out to meet him. Then all those virgins arose, and trimmed their lamps. And the foolish said unto the wise, Give us of your oil; for our lamps are gone out. But the wise answered, saying, *Not so*; lest there be not enough for us and you: but go ye rather to them that sell, and buy for yourselves. And while they went to buy, the bridegroom came; and they that were ready went in with him to the marriage: and the door was shut. Afterward came also the other virgins, saying, Lord, Lord, open to us. But he answered and said, Verily I say unto you, I know you not. Watch therefore, for ye know neither the day nor the hour wherein the Son of man cometh. (Matthew 25:1–13)

The parable of the ten virgins pictures the church waiting for the Bridegroom's return. Because of an unexpectedly long delay, He finds half the virgins unprepared when He finally arrives.

In weddings of that time, the bridegroom traditionally led a procession of bridesmaids from where they waited to his home. Since the procession almost invariably took place at night, each bridesmaid was expected to supply her own torch or lamp. If the bridegroom came later than expected, the bridesmaid needed to be prepared with extra torches or oil for her lamp.

The difference between the wise and the foolish virgins in the parable is not that one group did not have oil, but that one group did not have *enough* for the unexpectedly long delay. When the cry went out, their lamps were still burning, but they were sputtering and going out. Oil, of course, represents God's **Holy Spirit**. The wise virgins, like the faithful and wise servant, are prepared. They make sure that they remain in contact with the dispenser of oil, as is implied when they say to the foolish virgins, "No, ... go rather to those who sell, and buy for yourselves" (verse 9). The wise had been in recent contact with the dispenser of oil, whereas the others apparently had dallied around. Going frequently to the dispenser, the wise, when the bridegroom arrived, had an adequate supply to trim their lamps and go into the marriage supper. *The lesson is preparedness through vision and foresight.*

Because it is an internal state, preparedness cannot be transferred. That is evident in the reaction of the virgins. It is a matter of the heart, an intangible that accrues by spending long periods of time under many circumstances with the Dispenser of the Holy Spirit. What cannot be transferred to those who are unprepared are matters of attitude, character, skill, knowledge, understanding and **wisdom**. They are personal attributes that are built and honed over months and years.

When one needs a skill immediately, how much time does it take to learn it? If a man suddenly needed the skill to repair an automobile, and he had never done any work on one, he may as well have no hands at all! It works the same way with spiritual attributes. Preparing for eventualities is the lesson of this parable. The wise virgins prepared for the eventuality that it might take longer for the bridegroom to come—they showed foresight and vision, and they entered the wedding feast. The others did not.

The oil cannot be borrowed either. In no way can it be passed from one person to another. We cannot borrow character or a relationship with **God**. The parable teaches us that opportunity comes, opportunity knocks and then opportunity leaves. The foolish failed to face the possibility that the bridegroom would come later than expected, and when they were awakened, they had no time to fetch any oil and fill their lamps.

No one can deliver his brother. Each person determines his own destiny. No matter how close we are, even if we are one in flesh as in marriage, a husband cannot deliver his wife, and a wife cannot deliver her husband. Nor can we deliver our children. Everyone stands on his own in his relationship with God. God makes this clear in **Ezekiel 14:14**: **"'Though these three men, Noah, Daniel, and Job, were in it, they would deliver only themselves by their righteousness,' says the Lord God."** Though it is a hard lesson, it should motivate us to discipline ourselves, to exercise self-control, to be alert and to give our attention to our spiritual priorities. Thus, each person determines his own destiny.

Equating the foolish virgins with their modern counterparts [the **Laodiceans**], their **faith** is perfunctory. Their church membership is routine, merely going through the motions. They have enough faith that they at least show up for church services. They have beliefs and character and motivation—but not enough!

<u>**The Bridegroom's refusal to admit the five foolish virgins … must not be construed as a callous rejection of their lifelong desire to enter the Kingdom. … Far from callous, Christ's rejection is entirely justified because these people never make preparations for their marriage to Him. In the analogy, though they realize they have met their future mate and admire Him, they never develop the relationship. In a sense, they have already rejected Him. Thus, an additional lesson in this parable is that** *our relationship with God must be worked on continually.*</u> John W. Ritenbaugh (Bible Tools, https://1ref.us/tf, [accessed August 19, 2019], bold and underline print added)

Because of its abundance of well-known symbols, the **Parable of the Ten Virgins** is perhaps the easiest to understand in a prophetic light. The Bridegroom, of course, is Christ. Virgins are often symbols of churches or individual Christians, most likely the latter in this case. Lamps are vessels that contain oil, a common symbol of God's Spirit, thus they represent our minds, which, when filled with the **Holy Spirit**, provide illumination for the path to the **Kingdom of God (I Corinthians 2:10–16)**. The wedding refers to the marriage of the Lamb to the church (**Revelation 19:7**).

Jesus flatly states that this parable deals with conditions just before His **second coming** (verse 13). It does not take much interpretation, then, to understand what will happen—maybe has happened in part. All of God's people will go to sleep spiritually, but only half of them have enough spiritual strength to prepare for Christ's return. When He does return, our Savior shuts the door on the other half, proclaiming that He has no relationship with them (compare Revelation 3:7, 20). The warning to us is to draw close to **God** now because we do not know when Christ will come back. (Bible Tools, https://1ref.us/tg, [accessed August 19, 2019], bold print added)

Chapter 14—The Ephod and the Breastplate

According to the Bible, the onyx stones were to be placed in the ephod, which was covered by the High Priest's breastplate that had twelve precious stones. On the two onyx stones were engraved the names of the twelve tribes of Israel according to the births of the twelve sons of Jacob (later named Israel, which means "**God prevails**"). The onyx stones are the same two stones known in the Bible as the Urim and Thummim, by which God made His will known to the nation.

> At the right and left of the breastplate were two large stones of great brilliancy. These were known as the Urim and Thummim. By them the will of God was made known through the high priest. When questions were brought for decision before the Lord, a halo of light encircling the precious stone at the right was a token of the divine consent or approval, while a cloud shadowing the stone at the left was an evidence of denial or disapprobation. (White, *Patriarchs and Prophets*, p. 351)

In these last days of earth's history in which we are living, it is not only a good idea, but imperative for us to know what God's will is and isn't in accordance with our heavenly Father's plan for us. Many times, we are very quick to run ahead of God just as ancient Israel did, and just as the results were hardly ever favorable for them, so it is the same with us. We are even told that **"Now all these things happened unto them for examples: and they are written for our admonition, upon whom the ends of the world are come"** (1 Corinthians 10:11).

In these last days of earth's history in which we are living, it is not only a good idea, but imperative for us to know what God's will is and isn't in accordance with our heavenly Father's plan for us.

Therefore, we need to be on our knees more than ever before, praying and pleading with the Lord to make known to us what He would have us do on a daily basis. When He doesn't make known or reveal to us immediately what His will is in a given situation, we shouldn't get upset or become easily discouraged or disappointed. On the contrary, we should do as the Scriptures admonish us to do:

> **Trust in the LORD, and do good; *so* shalt thou dwell in the land, and verily thou shalt be fed. Delight thyself also in the LORD; and he shall give thee the desires of thine heart. Commit thy way unto the LORD; trust also in him; and he shall bring *it* to pass. And he shall bring forth thy righteousness as the light, and thy judgment as the noonday. Rest in the LORD, and wait patiently for him. (Psalm 37:3–7)**
>
> **Trust in the LORD with all thine heart; and lean not unto thine own understanding. In all thy ways acknowledge him, and he shall direct thy paths. (Proverbs 3:5, 6)**

What was the purpose of Aaron wearing the breastplate, with the twelve stones in it, over his chest?

> The Lord's direction was, "Aaron shall bear the names of the children of Israel in the breastplate of judgment upon his heart, when he goeth in unto the holy place, for a memorial before the Lord continually." Exodus 28:29. So Christ, the great High Priest, pleading His blood before the Father in the sinner's behalf, bears upon His heart the name of every repentant, believing soul. Says the psalmist, "I am poor and needy; yet the Lord thinketh upon me." Psalm 40:17. (White, *Patriarchs and Prophets*, p. 351)

What was the purpose of the miter that the high priest wore?

> The miter of the high priest consisted of the white linen turban, having attached to it by a lace of blue, a gold plate bearing the inscription, "Holiness to Jehovah." Everything connected with the apparel and deportment of the priests was to be such as to impress the beholder with a sense of the holiness of God, the sacredness of His worship, and the purity required of those who came into His presence.
>
> Not only the sanctuary itself, but the ministration of the priests, was to "serve unto the example and shadow of heavenly things." Hebrews 8:5. Thus it was of great importance; and the Lord, through Moses, gave the most definite and explicit instruction concerning every point of this typical service. The ministration of the

sanctuary consisted of two divisions, a daily and a yearly service. The daily service was performed at the altar of burnt offering in the court of the tabernacle and in the holy place; while the yearly service was in the most holy. (White, *Patriarchs and Prophets*, pp. 351, 352)

What was the purpose of the morning and evening sacrifices in the ancient sanctuary service?

Every morning and evening a lamb of a year old was burned upon the altar, with its appropriate meat offering, thus symbolizing the daily consecration of the nation to Jehovah, and their constant dependence upon the atoning blood of Christ. God expressly directed that every offering presented for the service of the sanctuary should be "without blemish." Exodus 12:5. The priests were to examine all animals brought as a sacrifice, and were to reject every one in which a defect was discovered. Only an offering "without blemish" could be a symbol of His perfect purity who was to offer Himself as "a lamb without blemish and without spot." 1 Peter 1:19. The apostle Paul points to these sacrifices as an illustration of what the followers of Christ are to become. He says, "I beseech you therefore, brethren, by the mercies of God, that ye present your bodies a living sacrifice, holy, acceptable unto God, which is your reasonable service." Romans 12:1. We are to give ourselves to the service of God, and we should seek to make the offering as nearly perfect as possible. God will not be pleased with anything less than the best we can offer. Those who love Him with all the heart, will desire to give Him the best service of the life, and they will be constantly seeking to bring every power of their being into harmony with the laws that will promote their ability to do His will. (White, *Patriarchs and Prophets*, pp. 352, 353)

Bibliography

Ritenbaugh, John W. "The World, the Church, and Laodiceanism." Bible Tools. https://1ref.us/tf (accessed August 19, 2019).

Ritenbaugh, Richard T. "Parables and Prophecy." Bible Tools. https://1ref.us/tg (accessed August 19, 2019).

White, Ellen G. *The Adventist Home*. Hagerstown, MD: Review and Herald Publishing Association, 1952.

———. *Christ Triumphant*. Hagerstown, MD: Review and Herald Publishing Association, 1999.

———. *Christ's Object Lessons*. Washington, DC: Review and Herald Publishing Association, 1900.

———. *The Desire of Ages*. Mountain View, CA: Pacific Press Publishing Association, 1898.

———. *God's Amazing Grace*. Washington, DC: Review and Herald Publishing Association, 1973.

———. *The Great Controversy*. Mountain View, CA: Pacific Press Publishing Association, 1911.

———. *Maranatha*. Washington, DC: Review and Herald Publishing Association, 1976.

———. *Our Father Cares*. Hagerstown, MD: Review and Herald Publishing Association, 1991.

———. *Patriarchs and Prophets*. Washington, DC: Review and Herald Publishing Association, 1890.

———. *Prophets and Kings*. Mountain View, CA: Pacific Press Publishing Association, 1917.

TEACH Services, Inc.
P U B L I S H I N G

We invite you to view the complete
selection of titles we publish at:
www.TEACHServices.com

We encourage you to write us
with your thoughts about this,
or any other book we publish at:
info@TEACHServices.com

TEACH Services' titles may be purchased in
bulk quantities for educational, fund-raising,
business, or promotional use.
bulksales@TEACHServices.com

Finally, if you are interested in seeing
your own book in print, please contact us at:
publishing@TEACHServices.com
We are happy to review your manuscript at no charge.

www.ingramcontent.com/pod-product-compliance
Lightning Source LLC
Chambersburg PA
CBHW042133160426
43199CB00021B/2899